How
Christians
Grow

In Beginning English
J. Wesley Eby
Editor

Beacon Hill Press of Kansas City
Kansas City, Missouri, U.S.A.

Copyright 1988, 2003
by Beacon Hill Press of Kansas City

ISBN 083-412-0593

Printed in the United States of America

Cover Design: Paul Franitza

10 9 8 7 6 5 4 3 2 1

CONTENTS

Acknowledgments		4
Introduction		5

Lesson No.   Lesson Title

1	You Can Grow as a Christian	6
2	Christians Should Be Baptized	8
3	Bible Study Helps Christians Grow	10
4	Prayer Helps Christians Grow	12
5	Christians Grow by Giving to God	14
6	Christians Serve God and Other People	16
7	Christians Should Be Good Witnesses	18
8	Christians Do What God Wants	20
9	The Holy Spirit Helps Us	22
10	A Christian Gives His Will to God	24
11	A Christian Can Be True to God	26
12	The Lord's Supper Is for Christians	28
13	God Heals People	30
14	Christians Enjoy Fellowship	32
15	Worship Helps Christians Grow	34
16	Christians Should Join a Church	36
17	Christians Grow in the Family of God	38

Teaching Resources	40
Appendix A: Word List: New Vocabulary	41
Appendix B: Answers to Questions and Additional Scripture References	44
Appendix C: Tips for Teaching ESL	53

Acknowledgments

We gratefully acknowledge the dedicated work of the following people who were involved in the writing of this book:

Roberta Eby, teacher (Kansas, U.S.A.)
Diana Haworth, nurse and former missionary to Latin America (Kansas, U.S.A.)
Rev. Will Haworth, pastor and former missionary to Latin America (Kansas, U.S.A.)
Cora Mae Jewell, college professor (Pennsylvania, U.S.A.)
Vicky Marty, high school teacher (Maryland, U.S.A.)
Ruth Rawlings, college professor and missionary (Japan)
Rev. Bill Rigel, pastor (Missouri, U.S.A.)
Lois J. Rigel, teacher (Missouri, U.S.A.)
Richard Stahl, Sr., school administrator (Delaware, U.S.A.)
Rita LaNell Stahl, high school teacher (Delaware, U.S.A.)
Nancy Zumwalt, educator and missionary (Taiwan)

We also deeply appreciate the numerous theologians and practitioners who carefully critiqued the lessons, providing much helpful advice and many practical suggestions.

Bennett Dudney, *Director*
Publications International

J. Wesley Eby, *ESL Editor*
Publications International

INTRODUCTION

This book is for people who are learning English. The words and sentences are short. This should help you understand the lessons.

The writers want you to know about God. They want you to know about living for God. And, they want you to understand what you are learning. This is why the book was written.

In this book, you will learn how Christians grow. You will learn about baptism. You will learn about Bible study and prayer. You will learn about the Holy Spirit. You will learn about living a holy life. You will learn many things about the Christian way.

Your pastor or teacher will help you learn. They want you to know about God. They want you to understand how Christians grow. So ask them for help. Ask them about the things you do not know. Ask them about the things you do not understand.

God loves you very much. He wants to be your God. He wants you to learn about Him. You can pray to God. You can ask Him to help you. He will help you understand. He will help you learn.

1 YOU CAN GROW AS A CHRISTIAN

Scripture: 2 Peter 3:18

You are now a Christian. This is **wonderful!** You have made the most important **decision** of your life!

Or it may be that you are not a Christian yet. But, you can be. You can choose Jesus Christ as your own Savior. You can do it now! Ask your pastor or teacher to help you.

A new believer needs to learn about the Christian life. He or she needs to understand more about living a holy life. These lessons are to help Christians grow.

We have learned about God and His plans for us. We have learned that we worship the one true God. He created our world and He lives forever. God is holy and loving. He hears and answers our prayers. He is a **triune** God. Through Jesus Christ, God shows us who He is.

We have learned that the Bible tells us about God. It tells us about good and bad people. It tells us how God forgives our sins. It tells us how to live in a **difficult world.**

We have learned that God will judge us after death. We will go to hell if we are sinners. We will go to heaven if we are Christians. God wants us to live in heaven with Him.

We have learned that Jesus Christ is God. He came to earth. He showed us how to live. He died as the sacrifice for our sins. Then, He came back to life after He died. Believers are looking for Jesus Christ to come again.

Now, we will learn more about living the Christian life. We will learn more about the Holy Spirit. And we will also learn about our church life.

Yes, we can grow as Christians. God wants us to grow. The Bible says, ". . . grow in the . . . **knowledge** of . . . Jesus Christ. . . ." (2 Peter 3:18)

QUESTIONS: *Fill in the blanks.*

1. A new believer needs to _____ about the Christian life.
2. We worship the one _____ God.
3. God hears and _____ our prayers.
4. The _____ tells us about God.
5. We will go to hell if we are _____.
6. We will go to _____ if we are Christians.
7. We learned that Jesus Christ is _____.
8. _____ are looking for Jesus Christ to come again.

Answer YES or NO. Circle the right answer for you.

9. Are you a Christian?   YES or NO
10. Is Jesus Christ your Savior right now?   YES or NO
11. Do you want to learn about the Christian life?   YES or NO
12. Do you want to grow as a Christian?   YES or NO

WORD LIST

1. **grow as a Christian** *(verb phrase):* to learn more about the Christian life; to be more like Jesus Christ
2. **wonderful** *(adjective):* great; very, very good
3. **decision** *(noun):* what you decide to do; what you choose to do
4. **triune** *(adjective):* God is God in three persons: God the Father, God the Son, and God the Holy Spirit
5. **difficult world** *(noun phrase):* not easy to live in; hard to live in; a world full of sin and wrong
6. **knowledge** *(noun):* what a person knows; what a person has learned

2 CHRISTIANS SHOULD BE BAPTIZED

Scripture: Matthew 28:19

Jesus Christ taught His **disciples** to baptize believers. He said, ". . . go and make disciples . . . baptizing them . . ." (Matthew 28:19)

Baptism is for all Christians. It is for all people who believe in Jesus Christ. It is for people who repent of their sins. They must believe that Jesus Christ is their Savior. Baptism shows they belong to Jesus Christ.

Baptism shows that we turn away from all sin. It shows that God has **saved** us from sin. It shows a **separation** from the life of sin. The Bible says, ". . . we should no longer be **slaves to sin**." (Romans 6:6) Baptism shows we have begun the Christian life.

Water is used for baptism. Many Christians are dipped into water. Some Christians have water poured on their heads. Other Christians have water **sprinkled** on their heads. These are three ways people are baptized.

A **minister** baptizes Christians. He baptizes ". . . in the name of the Father . . . Son and . . . Holy Spirit." (Matthew 28:19)

We should be baptized where other people can watch. This shows them that we believe in Jesus Christ. It shows that we have chosen the Christian way.

We should be baptized after we are saved. We obey what the Bible teaches when we are baptized. Baptism helps us grow as Christians.

QUESTIONS: Fill in the blanks.

1. Baptism is for people who _____ of their sins.
2. Baptism shows a separation from the life of _____.
3. Baptism shows that God has _____ us from sin.
4. Baptism shows other people that we _____ in

    _____ _____.
5. We obey what the Bible says when we are _____.

Give the answers.

6. Who told us to be baptized? _____ _____
7. Who is baptism for? _____ _____
8. Who should baptize us? _____ _____
9. Where should we be baptized? Where other people

    _____ _____.

WORD LIST

1. **disciples** *(noun):* believers; people who follow Jesus Christ
2. **saved** *(verb):* made free or safe from sin; freed from the power of sin in our lives
3. **separation** *(noun):* not together; apart
4. **slaves to sin** *(noun phrase):* people who are sinners; people who are controlled by sin
5. **sprinkled** *(verb):* shake small drops of water on
6. **minister** *(noun):* a preacher who serves God and people in the church

3 BIBLE STUDY HELPS CHRISTIANS GROW

Scripture: 2 Timothy 3:16

The Holy Bible is called the Word of God. God speaks to us through the Bible.

Christians need to grow and know God better. The Bible can help us. It can help us grow as Christians. It can help us know God better. It can help us learn how to obey God.

We should read and study the Bible every day. Then, we will grow. We will become better Christians.

Here are some ways the Bible helps us as Christians:

1. The Bible leads to life in Jesus Christ. He said, "The words I have spoken . . . are life." (John 6:63) Jesus Christ gives us **eternal life.**
2. The Bible helps us know the truth. Jesus Christ said, "I am . . . the truth . . ." (John 14:6) He also said the truth makes us free. Bible study helps us know the truth. The truth frees us from sin.
3. The Bible shows us the sin and wrong in our lives. It helps us make right **choices.** It teaches us how to live right. "All Scripture is useful for teaching . . ." (2 Timothy 3:16)
4. The Bible gives us good **spiritual** food. People need food every day to live. People eat good food and are **healthy.** Christians also need spiritual food every day. The Christian life must be fed. Bible study is one way that Christians are fed. Bible study helps us to be healthy Christians.

Christians should start Bible study with prayer. We should ask God for help. He will help us understand the things that we read. God will help us understand the Bible. The Holy Spirit will teach us.

We should make the Holy Bible important in our lives. We should listen to God while we study His Word. Then, we should obey Him. We become better Christians as we obey God. We grow as we study the Bible.

QUESTIONS: *Fill in the blanks.*

1. God speaks to Christians through the _____.
2. The Bible can help us know _____ _____ .
3. Christians should _____ and _____
   the Bible every day.
4. The Bible helps us know the _____.
5. The Bible teaches us how to _____ right.

Give the answers.

6. What do we become as we study the Bible? _____
   _____.
7. Who is truth? _____ _____
8. What does the Bible show us about our lives? _____
   and _____
9. Who helps us understand the Bible? _____
10. What book is important for Christians? _____

WORD LIST

1. **Bible study** *(noun phrase):* learning what is in the Bible; learning what the Bible says to us
2. **eternal life** *(noun phrase):* the life God gives; the good life with God now and life with God forever
3. **choices** *(noun):* acts of choosing or deciding something; when we decide between two or more things
4. **spiritual** *(adjective):* things of God; things of the Holy Spirit
5. **healthy** *(adjective):* not sick; being well in the body

4 PRAYER HELPS CHRISTIANS GROW

Scripture: Romans 12:12

Prayer is talking with God. People can talk with God. We talk with God like we talk with people. And God listens when we pray.

We pray with our words and thoughts. We can use our own words. We can use words from the Bible. Or we can use words of **hymns** or written prayers.

We can pray alone. Or we can pray with other people. We can pray in church or at home. We can pray at any time or in any place.

God wants us to pray. This is one reason we pray. The Bible says, "Be . . . **faithful** in prayer." (Romans 12:12) God loves us very much. God wants us to talk with Him.

Prayer is a special way to give love to God. We praise and thank God. We praise Him for who He is. We thank Him for His gifts to us. We praise and thank Him for His love.

We pray to God because we love Him. We talk with people we love. We tell them we love them. We tell them about our problems. We also want to tell God we love Him. We tell Him our problems.

We can tell God about our needs in prayer. The Bible says, "Ask and it will be given to you . . ." (Matthew 7:7) God will **supply** our needs. He wants to give us good things. But God wants us to ask Him for these things.

We pray to God for **forgiveness.** We ask God to forgive us for our sins. God will forgive us. He answers the **honest** prayer for forgiveness.

God answers our prayers. He said, "Call to Me and I will answer you . . ." (Jeremiah 33:3) Sometimes God answers "yes." Sometimes He answers "no." And sometimes He answers "wait." God knows what is best for us. His answer is always right.

God will help us learn to pray. Jesus Christ taught us how to pray. Read His prayer in the Bible. (Matthew 6:9-13) It is called the Lord's Prayer. You should **memorize** it and pray it often.

We love God more as we pray. Prayer helps us become better Christians. It helps us grow as Christians.

QUESTIONS: *Fill in the blanks.*

1. _____ is talking with God.
2. We pray with our _____ and _____.
3. Prayer is a special way to give love to _____.
4. The Bible says, "Ask and it will be _____
   _____ _____."
5. God answers the honest prayer for _____.
6. God answers our _____. His answer is always
   _____.

Give the answers.

7. When can we pray? _____ _____ _____
8. What will God supply? _____ _____
9. Who will forgive us? _____
10. Jesus Christ taught us how to pray. What is His prayer called?

   _____ _____

WORD LIST

1. **hymns** *(noun):* songs that praise and worship God
2. **faithful** *(adjective):* always doing what you should be doing; full of faith
3. **supply** *(verb):* give what is needed
4. **forgiveness** *(noun):* God choosing to forgive our sins
5. **honest** *(adjective):* true; right
6. **memorize** *(verb):* learn something so you can remember it

5 CHRISTIANS GROW BY GIVING TO GOD

Scripture: 2 Corinthians 9:7

God loves His people. He wants them to grow. He knows Christians grow by serving Him. And God tells us in the Bible how to serve Him.

One way to serve God is to give a **tithe.** A tithe is one part of ten. For **example,** one dollar is a tithe of ten dollars. The Bible says, "Bring the whole tithe into the **storehouse** . . ." (Malachi 3:10) The storehouse means the church. Or it means the place where you worship God.

God tells all Christians to tithe. Christians should tithe because it belongs to God. The Bible says, "A tithe . . . belongs to the Lord . . ." (Leviticus 27:30)

Christians should also give **offerings** because they love God. God gives so very much to His children. Everything we have comes from Him. And He gave His Son to die for our sins. We should want to give to God.

Christians should be happy **givers.** The Bible says, ". . . God loves a **cheerful** giver." (2 Corinthians 9:7) We should be full of joy as we give. This is one way we can thank God.

Christians should give time to God. This is another way we can serve Him. We pray and study the Bible every day. We go to church. We **witness** to other people and we help them. These are some of the ways we give our time.

Christians should also give their **talents** to God. All people can do certain things very well. These things are called talents. Our talents should be used to serve God. We should give our talents to God.

Yes, we grow as we give to God. We become strong Christians as we give. We become strong because we obey God. And God promises to **bless** us as we obey Him.

QUESTIONS: *Fill in the blanks.*

1. God knows that Christians grow by _____ Him.
2. One way to serve God is to give a _____.
3. Christians should give offerings because they _____

   _____.

4. We become strong Christians as we _____ to God.
5. Four things we should give to God are our _____,

   _____, _____, and _____.

Give the answers.

6. What does "storehouse" mean? _____ _____
7. Whom does the tithe belong to? _____
8. What kind of a giver should Christians be? _____
9. What do we call the certain things we do very well?

   Our _____
10. What are three ways you can give time to God?

    (1) _____
    (2) _____
    (3) _____

WORD LIST

1. **tithe** *(noun):* one part of ten; money given to God through the church
2. **example** *(noun):* shows one of a kind of something; an example helps us to know better what something means or is
3. **storehouse** *(noun):* the church or place where you worship God
4. **offerings** *(noun):* gifts given to God, usually money
5. **givers** *(noun):* people who give something; people who give money to God
6. **cheerful** *(adjective):* happy; glad
7. **witness** *(verb):* tell people about Jesus Christ; tell what Jesus Christ has done for you
8. **talents** *(noun):* the things people do very well; what people are able to do very well
9. **bless** *(verb):* make happy; give joy to

6 CHRISTIANS SERVE GOD AND OTHER PEOPLE

Scripture: Matthew 4:10

Christians are **servants** of God. The Bible says, ". . . Worship the Lord your God, and serve Him only." (Matthew 4:10) Christians serve God by serving other people. Christians do not serve God for money. They serve God because they love Him.

The Bible tells us Jesus Christ came to serve people. ". . . the **Son of Man** did not come to be served, but to serve . . ." (Mark 10:45)

Jesus Christ is our best example of a servant. He helped many people. Some people were sick and sad. Other people were hungry and **lonely.** Jesus Christ loved and helped them.

We can serve God in many ways. In the last lesson, we learned about giving to God. We serve God when we give to Him. We serve God when we give our tithes and offerings. We serve God when we give Him our time. And, we serve God when we give Him our talents.

We can serve God in many places. We can serve Him at church. Our ministers are servants of God. People who help with music are servants of God. Teachers and **janitors** are servants, too.

We can serve God away from church. Some people have Bible studies in their homes. Some people cook meals for other people. Some Christians care for sick people.

Some people visit **non-Christians** and witness to them. Some Christians help poor or lonely people. Some people are kind to their **enemies.** The Bible says, ". . . serve one another in love." (Galatians 5:13)

God can tell us how to serve Him. He can help us know what we should do. God can show us how to be His servants. We grow as we serve God.

QUESTIONS: *Fill in the blanks.*

1. Christians are _____ of God.
2. The Bible tells us that Jesus Christ came to _____.
3. We can serve God in _____ _____.
4. We can serve God at _____. We can serve God _____ from church.

Give the answers.

5. Why do Christians serve God? Because _____ _____ _____.

6. Who is our best example of a servant? _____ _____

7. What are three ways to serve God away from church?

    (1) _____.
    (2) _____.
    (3) _____.

8. Who shows us how to serve? _____

WORD LIST

1. **servants** *(noun):* people who serve God and other people; people who work for God
2. **Son of Man** *(proper noun phrase):* Jesus Christ
3. **lonely** *(adjective):* feeling all alone; feeling no one cares about you
4. **janitors** *(noun):* people who clean and take care of buildings
5. **non-Christians** *(noun):* people who are not Christians; people who do not believe in Jesus Christ
6. **enemies** *(noun):* people who are not friends; people who hate and hurt other people

7 CHRISTIANS SHOULD BE GOOD WITNESSES

Scripture: Acts 1:8

All of us have nice things happen to us. These things make us very happy. And we like to share our **happiness** with someone else. We like to share our good news. This is called **witnessing.**

A new baby gives us joy to share. We like to tell about a new home. We like to share nice surprises. But news about Jesus Christ is the best news of all. This is the best news that Christians can share. Jesus Christ said, ". . . you will be My witnesses . . ." (Acts 1:8)

Christians should share what God has done for them. A Christian has forgiveness for sins. A Christian has been saved from sin. He or she wants to share this good news.

Other people need to know who can forgive sins. This person is Jesus Christ. He wants to save them from sin, too. This is the good news of the **gospel.** We witness when we share the gospel.

We also witness for God by what we do. We witness by both our acts and our words. People hear what we say. They also see the things we do. It is important to live for God all the time.

Christians must be good witnesses, not bad witnesses. Christians should be kind to everyone. They should speak kind words. They should do good things for all people.

Christians may not like the things other people do. They may not like how others live. But Christians should remember to be kind. Jesus Christ said, ". . . all men will know that you are My disciples, if you love one another." (John 13:35) Christians do not want to hurt other people.

Sometimes, Christians hurt other people. But God helps us to know this. We must ask God to forgive us when we hurt people. We must ask people to forgive us when we hurt them. True disciples want to be good witnesses.

Christians are sometimes afraid to witness. But Jesus Christ said, ". . . Do not be afraid. Go and tell . . ." (Matthew 28:10) He also said, ". . . I am with you always . . ." (Matthew 28:20) We do not need to be afraid. Jesus Christ has promised to be with us.

Christians need to be good witnesses for God. We need to share the good news of the gospel. We grow and become strong Christians when we witness.

QUESTIONS: *Fill In the blanks.*

1. The best news Christians can share is about _____

   _____.

2. A Christian has _____ for sins.

3. Jesus Christ said, ". . . all men will know that you are My

   _____, if you _____ one another."

4. True disciples want to be good _____.

5. Christians are sometimes _____ to witness.

Give the answers.

6. What should Christians share? What God has _____

   _____ _____.

7. How do we witness for God? By our _____ and by

   our _____.

8. Who is with us always? _____ _____

9. What type of witnesses must Christians be? _____
   (See the lesson title.)

WORD LIST

1. **happiness** *(noun):* being happy and glad; full of joy
2. **witnessing** *(noun):* sharing or telling other people about something good; telling other people about God and His Son, Jesus Christ
3. **gospel** *(noun):* the story of salvation from sin through Jesus Christ; this story is told in Matthew, Mark, Luke, and John; these four books are called the Gospels

8 CHRISTIANS DO WHAT GOD WANTS

Scripture: 1 Thessalonians 5:22

We have learned that Christians listen to God. Christians pray and study the Holy Bible. God teaches us how we should live. He uses many ways to teach us. He uses many ways to help us grow.

We should live to **please** God. Sinners do things that do not please Him. But, God changes how we live when we become Christians. We **avoid** things that do not please God. The Bible says, "Avoid every kind of evil." (1 Thessalonians 5:22)

The Bible tells us things we should avoid. The Bible also tells us many things we should do. The **Ten Commandments** help us. The words of Jesus Christ help us. We must listen to God and obey His Word.

Christians use the name of God with care. The name of God is **sacred** and holy. We must not use His name in the wrong way. (Exodus 20:7) Christians also keep the **Lord's Day** holy. It is a day to **honor** God. (Exodus 20:8)

Christians avoid anything that will hurt their bodies. Our bodies are the **temples** for the Holy Spirit. We must avoid **sex sins.** We do not put anything into our bodies that is **harmful.** We honor God by keeping our bodies pure. (Exodus 20:14; 1 Corinthians 6:18-20)

Christians want to please God in everything. We read and watch things that please Him. We avoid places that are harmful. We avoid anything that would make God sad. (1 Corinthians 10:31; 1 John 2:15-16)

Jesus Christ shows us how we should love people. We, too, should love everyone. We should not fight people with our hands. We should not fight them with our words. We should not hurt people. We must not make them sorry they know us. (Mark 12:31; 2 Corinthians 12:20)

Christians should honor God. We honor Him with our bodies and minds. We honor Him with our words and deeds. We avoid anything that makes us sin. Christians want to live holy, pure lives. This helps us to grow as Christians.

QUESTIONS: *Fill in the blanks.*

1. We should live to _____ _____.

2. Christians use the _____ _____ _____ with care.

3. Christians avoid anything that will _____ their bodies.

4. Christians want to please God in _____.

5. Christians want to live _____, _____ lives.

Give the answers.

6. What are we to avoid? Things that _____ _____
_____ _____.

7. What tells us the things we should avoid? _____ _____

8. What day do Christians keep holy? _____ _____ _____

9. Who shows us how we should love people? _____
_____

10. How do Christians honor God? With our _____ and
_____; with our _____ and _____.

WORD LIST

1. **please** *(verb):* to make someone happy; to make God happy
2. **avoid** *(verb):* keep away from; not do at all
3. **Ten Commandments** *(proper noun phrase):* ten important laws or rules that God gave to His people (See Exodus 20:2-17)
4. **sacred** *(adjective):* belongs to God; holy
5. **Lord's Day** *(proper noun phrase):* Sunday; the day most Christians worship God
6. **honor** *(verb):* worship; obey; give a high place to
7. **temples** *(noun):* places of worship; places where the Spirit of God lives
8. **sex sins** *(noun phrase):* wrong sex; all sex that is not between a man and his wife
9. **harmful** *(adjective):* full of harm; that which hurts us; that which makes us sin

9 THE HOLY SPIRIT HELPS US

Scripture: John 14:26

Christians believe that God is triune. He is three in one. God is the Father. He is the Son, Jesus Christ. And He is the Holy Spirit.

The Holy Spirit works in the lives of all people. He is everywhere. He does the work of God in our lives.

The Holy Spirit is a **counselor.** The Bible says, ". . . the Counselor, the Holy Spirit, . . . will teach you all things . . ." (John 14:26) The Holy Spirit helps us with our problems. He teaches us what we should learn.

The Holy Spirit works in the lives of sinners. He shows sinners their need for God. Jesus Christ said, ". . . He [the Counselor] will **convict** the world of . . . sin . . ." (John 16:8) He helps sinners to know about their sins.

The Holy Spirit works in the life of every Christian. The Bible says, ". . . the Holy Spirit . . . is in you . . ." (1 Corinthians 6:19) He is God living inside us. He is in our hearts. He helps us grow as Christians.

Christians are the children of God. The Holy Spirit helps us know this. "The **Spirit** . . . **testifies** with our **spirit** that we are God's children." (Romans 8:16)

The Holy Spirit is the Spirit of truth. He teaches us the truth of God. Jesus Christ said, ". . . the Spirit of truth . . . will guide you into all truth. . . ." (John 16:13)

The Holy Spirit helps us with our sin problem. He helps us to have **victory over sin.** The Holy Spirit helps us to live holy lives. He helps us to grow.

QUESTIONS: *Give the answers.*

1. Who is the Father? _____
2. Who is the Son? _____ _____
3. Where does the Holy Spirit work? In the _____ of people.
4. Who is the Holy Spirit? A _____ (See John 14:26.)
5. What does the Holy Spirit help us with? Our _____
6. Who shows sinners their need for God? _____ _____
   _____
7. What will the Counselor do? He will _____ the world of _____. (See John 16:8.)
8. Who are the children of God? _____
9. Who helps us with our sin problem? _____ _____
   _____
10. What will the Holy Spirit help us have victory over? _____

WORD LIST

1. **counselor** *(noun):* a person who listens to our problems; a person who helps us with our problems
2. **convict** *(verb):* make known; help people to know about
3. **Spirit** *(proper noun):* the Holy Spirit; the Spirit of God
4. **testifies** *(verb):* makes us know; agrees with
5. **spirit** *(noun):* the real self; what a person is inside his being
6. **victory over sin** *(noun phrase):* have no sin; obey God in all things

10 A CHRISTIAN GIVES HIS WILL TO GOD

Scripture: 1 Thessalonians 5:23

God gave His best to us. He gave His Son, Jesus Christ, to save us from sin. Christians want to give their best to God. The best gift that we can give Him is our will.

Christians know the will of God is best for them. Christians want to do the **will of God.** They want to serve and obey Him. But this is not always easy to do.

Sometimes, we want our own way. We fight against the will of God. We want our own way more than we want the will of God.

Christians need to choose the will of God. The will of God should be more important than our will. We should choose to give our will to God. This important decision is called **consecration.**

The believer **consecrates** his will. Then the Holy Spirit **purifies** the believer. ". . . He [the Holy Spirit] purified their hearts . . ." (Acts 15:9) He takes from us all that fights against God. The Holy Spirit helps us love God **completely.**

The **consecrated** believer belongs completely to God. God **sanctifies** the believer. "May God . . . sanctify you **through and through**. . . ." (1 Thessalonians 5:23) One name for this act is **entire sanctification.**

The consecrated believer is filled with the Holy Spirit. "All of them were filled with the Holy Spirit . . ." (Acts 2:4) The Holy Spirit gives the believer special help. He helps believers to do the will of God.

All Christians must make a choice. They choose the will of God or their own will. They must choose the will of God. Or they stop growing as Christians.

Do you want to give your best to God? Do you want the will of God for your life? Do you need to consecrate your will to God? If so, you can pray this prayer of consecration:

Dear God, I give my will to You. I give my fears to You. I give everything I own to You. I give my family to You. And I give myself to You. Please accept my love for You. Fill me with Your Holy Spirit. Help me to obey You completely. Thank You, Father. In Jesus' name, I pray. Amen.

QUESTIONS: *Fill in the blanks.*

1. Christians want to give their _____ to God.
2. Sometimes, we want our own _____.
3. Christians need to _____ the will of God.
4. Consecration is choosing to give our _____ to God.
5. The _____ _____ purifies the believer.
6. The Holy Spirit helps us _____ _____ completely.
7. The _____ believer belongs completely to God.
8. "May God . . . _____ you through and through . . . "
9. The consecrated believer is _____ with the Holy Spirit.
10. The Holy Spirit helps believers to _____ the will of God.

WORD LIST

1. **will** *(noun):* the power to choose; to decide between two or more things
2. **will of God** *(noun phrase):* what God wants for people
3. **consecration** *(noun):* the act of giving something to God
4. **consecrates** *(verb):* gives something to God to be used only by God
5. **purifies** *(verb):* makes clean and pure; makes holy
6. **completely** *(adverb):* all; in whole; with everything
7. **consecrated** *(adjective):* given to God
8. **sanctifies** *(verb):* makes pure and holy; sets apart for a holy reason
9. **through and through** *(adverb phrase):* in whole; completely; from top to bottom; from one side to the other side
10. **entire sanctification** *(noun phrase):* the special act of God that makes Christians pure and holy; this happens after people are saved from sin
11. **myself** *(pronoun):* I; me

11 A CHRISTIAN CAN BE TRUE TO GOD

Scripture: 1 John 1:9

Every Christian is a child of God. God loves His children and helps them each day. He wants His children to love and obey Him. God wants His children to consecrate their wills to Him. And we want to love and obey God.

But we have many problems every day. These problems may stop us from growing as Christians. Sometimes we **neglect** the things we should do. For example, we may not pray and study the Bible. We may not witness. We may not serve God. We may not go to church.

This neglect begins to separate us from God. We begin losing **fellowship** with God. We do not feel close to God. We begin to **backslide.**

Sometimes it is difficult for us to obey God. All Christians are tempted to do wrong. Even Jesus Christ was tempted. But **temptation** is not sin. We sin only when we **yield** to the temptation.

Christians make a choice every time we are tempted. We choose the will of God. Or we choose our own will. If we choose our will, we sin. Sin is choosing our will, not the will of God. This is called **backsliding.**

But, Christians really love God. We do not want to lose our fellowship with Him. We do not want to backslide. We want to be true to God.

God wants to forgive us when we sin. But we must be sorry and repent of our sins. We must ask Him to forgive us. The Bible says, "If we confess our sins, He [God] . . . will forgive us our sins . . ." (1 John 1:9) Then we have close fellowship with God again.

Christians do not need to backslide. The Holy Spirit helps us to obey God. He helps us choose His will when we are tempted. "But when you are tempted, He [God] will also **provide a way out** . . ." (1 Corinthians 10:13) We grow more every time we choose the will of God.

QUESTIONS: *Fill In the blanks.*

1. Every Christian is a _____ _____ _____.
2. Sometimes we _____ the things we should do.
3. Neglect begins to _____ us from God. We begin losing _____ with God.
4. _____ is not sin.
5. We sin only when we _____ to temptation.
6. _____ is choosing our will, not the will of God.
7. God wants to _____ us when we sin.
8. Christians do not need to _____.
9. The _____ _____ will help us to obey God.

WORD LIST

1. **true** *(adjective):* faithful; always doing what you should be doing; always obeying God
2. **neglect** *(verb):* to not do; to not care for
3. **fellowship** *(noun):* being friends; loving and caring for each other
4. **backslide** *(verb):* to neglect doing the will of God; to choose to disobey God; to turn from following Jesus Christ
5. **temptation** *(noun):* the act of being tempted by Satan; Satan trying to get a person to do wrong and disobey God
6. **yield** *(verb):* to do the thing we should not do; to say "yes" to sin
7. **backsliding** *(noun):* neglecting to do the will of God; choosing our will, not the will of God; choosing not to follow Jesus Christ
8. **provide a way out** *(verb phrase):* make us strong; help us not to yield; help us not to sin

12 THE LORD'S SUPPER IS FOR CHRISTIANS

Scripture: 1 Corinthians 11:26

Christian churches have a special **service**. This service is called the Lord's Supper. The Lord's Supper is also called Communion.

The Lord's Supper is only for believers. During Communion, Jesus Christ is with us in a special way.

Jesus Christ lived on earth for about 33 years. He had 12 disciples. He lived with them and taught them. But Jesus knew He would die on the Cross. He knew He would soon leave the earth.

Jesus wanted His disciples to remember Him. He wanted them to remember the meaning of His death. So Jesus planned a special meal. It was His last supper before He died.

Jesus and the disciples were eating the meal. ". . . Jesus took bread, **gave thanks**, and broke it . . ." (Matthew 26:26) Jesus gave the bread to His disciples. He said, ". . . Take and eat; this is my body." (Matthew 26:26)

Next, Jesus took some juice made from grapes. He gave thanks. Then He gave the cup of juice to His disciples. He said, ". . . Drink from it, all of you. This is my blood . . . **poured out** . . . for the forgiveness of sins." (Matthew 26:27-28) This was the first Lord's Supper.

The Lord's Supper has two parts. Jesus used bread to **represent** His body. His body was **broken** on the Cross. Jesus used the juice to represent His blood. His blood was **shed** on the Cross.

During Communion, we remember the death of Jesus. We remember He died for all our sins. We remember that He is coming again. Jesus said, ". . . do this **in remembrance of** Me." (Luke 22:19) This is why it is a special time of worship. We are to do this until Jesus comes back.

Communion is a good time for us to pray. We can ask God to show us any sin or wrong. He can show us what He wants us to change. This is one way we can grow as Christians.

QUESTIONS: *Give the answers.*

1. What is another name for Communion? The _____

   _____

2. Who is the Lord's Supper for? _____

3. What words mean that Jesus prayed before He ate the meal?

   _____ _____

4. What did Jesus use to represent His body? _____

5. What did Jesus use to represent His blood? _____

6. What did Jesus shed on the Cross? _____

7. What do we remember when we take Communion?

   The _____ of _____.

8. How long are we to take Communion? Until Jesus Christ

   _____ _____.

WORD LIST

1. **service** *(noun):* a time when Christians meet together to worship God
2. **gave thanks** *(verb phrase):* prayed; thanked God for; prayed before eating a meal
3. **poured out** *(verb phrase):* given; spilled; shed
4. **represent** *(verb):* to mean; to show
5. **broken** *(verb):* hurt; death
6. **shed** *(verb):* given; spilled; poured out
7. **in remembrance of** *(prepositional phrase):* to remember; to think of again

13 GOD HEALS PEOPLE

Scripture: James 5:14

Sometimes people get sick. We do not like to be sick. We want to be well.

People get sick in many ways. Our bodies may be sick. Sometimes, our minds or **emotions** may not be well. But God helps us when we are sick.

Jesus Christ helped sick people when He was on earth. He healed sick people. The Bible says, ". . . Jesus . . . healed their sick." (Matthew 14:14)

Today, we can ask God to heal us. Sometimes we need others to pray for us. Our **pastor** is a good person to pray for us. The Bible says, "Is any one of you sick? He should call the **elders** of the church to pray over him . . ." (James 5:14)

God uses different ways to heal us. He can heal us by His great power. He can heal us **immediately.** Or sometimes God heals us **gradually.**

God also uses doctors to heal us. And He uses **medicine** to heal us. This healing may take more time.

Sometimes God does not choose to heal us. Our healing may not be His will for us. We may not understand this. But God understands. He always does what is best for us.

We can be well in our spirit when we are sick. **Sickness** does not mean that we are sinners. God still loves us and saves us from sin. We can live holy lives when we are sick.

God helps us when we are sick. He gives us the **strength** we need each day. The Bible says, "I can do everything through Him [God] who gives me strength." (Philippians 4:13)

QUESTIONS: *Fill in the blanks.*

1. Our _____ may be sick. Sometimes, our _____ or _____ may not be well.
2. Jesus Christ healed _____ _____.
3. God can heal us by His _____ _____.
4. God can _____ us immediately or gradually.
5. God also uses _____ and _____ to heal us.
6. Sometimes God does not _____ to heal us.
7. _____ does not mean we are sinners.

Give the answers.

8. Whom can we ask to heal us? _____
9. Who can pray for us when we are sick? The _____ and _____ of the church.
10. What can we do through the strength of God? _____

WORD LIST

1. **emotions** *(noun):* our feelings, such as love, hate, fear, joy, etc.
2. **pastor** *(noun):* the minister or preacher in a church
3. **elders** *(noun):* important leaders in a church
4. **immediately** *(adverb):* right away; done at once; happens with no waiting
5. **gradually** *(adverb):* slow change; not fast; not happening all at one time
6. **medicine** *(noun):* what doctors give to help make people well
7. **sickness** *(noun):* being sick; not well
8. **strength** *(noun):* power; help

14 CHRISTIANS ENJOY FELLOWSHIP

Scripture: 1 John 1:7

We like to be with our families and friends. They are special to us. We belong to each other. This is fellowship. We also feel this way about other Christians. This is Christian fellowship.

We have Christian fellowship when we worship God together. We pray for each other. We hear people **testify.** We learn how God helps them. We like being with each other. We become friends. They help us grow.

Christian fellowship is more than being friends. It is showing Christian love by **sharing and caring.** We help people when they need help.

Here are some ways we can help people:

1. We can give food to people who are hungry.
2. We can give clothing to people who need clothing.
3. We can help someone find a job.
4. We can help sick people. We can take them to the doctor. We can cook food for them or clean their house.
5. We can visit lonely people. We can send them a letter or a card. We can call them on the **telephone.**
6. We can help people who have lost someone by death. We can visit them. We can pray for them.

We are often with people who are not Christians. We must show them Christian love also. They will then know we care about them. They may become Christians because of our love and caring. They will learn what Christian fellowship is.

There is another type of fellowship. It is the love of God for His children. And it is the love His children have for Him. We can have this special fellowship with God **continually.**

Christians need fellowship with God. We should have a time for **devotions** each day. We feel God near when we pray to Him. He speaks to us when we read the Bible. We **feel His presence** when we worship Him. Then we grow as Christians.

The Bible teaches us about fellowship. ". . . our fellowship is with the Father and . . . Jesus Christ." (1 John 1:3) ". . . if we walk in the light . . . we have fellowship with one another . . ." (1 John 1:7) We must obey God to have fellowship with Him. Then we have fellowship with other people.

Christian fellowship is a gift to us from God. Let us thank Him for this special gift.

QUESTIONS: *Fill in the blanks.*

1. We have Christian _____ when we
   _____ God together.
2. We learn how God helps other people when they _____.
3. Christian fellowship is also showing Christian love by
   _____ and _____.
4. People who are not Christians may become Christians because
   of our _____ and _____.
5. We can have special fellowship with _____ continually.
6. We should take time for _____ every day.
7. We feel the _____ of God when we worship Him.

Give the answers.

8. What are three ways you can help people?
   (1) _____
   (2) _____
   (3) _____
9. Whom does the Bible say we have fellowship with? The
   _____ and _____ _____
10. What is a special gift to us from God? _____
    _____

WORD LIST

1. **testify** *(verb):* tell other people what God has done for you
2. **sharing and caring** *(noun phrase):* helping people; letting people
   know you want to help them in any way you can; giving to other
   people a part of what you have; being friends with people
3. **telephone** *(noun):* a tool we use to talk with people away from
   us; we can hear them but we cannot see them
4. **continually** *(adverb):* all the time; never stops
5. **devotions** *(noun):* a time of prayer, Bible study, and thinking
   about God
6. **feel His presence** *(verb phrase):* know God is present; know God
   is near

15 WORSHIP HELPS CHRISTIANS GROW

Scripture: Hebrews 10:25

Christians worship the one true God. We worship the triune God. The Bible says, ". . . Worship the Lord your God, and serve Him only." (Matthew 4:10)

People can worship many things. We can worship false gods. We can worship other people. We can worship money and our jobs. We can worship things we own. But this type of worship is not right.

We must worship only God. He said, "You shall have no other Gods before Me." (Exodus 20:3) This means that nothing should be more important than God. We sin when we put anything or anyone before Him.

We worship God in many ways. We worship when we give praise to God. We show Him **reverence.** We give Him our love. We give Him our lives. We tell God that only He is **worthy** of our worship.

We worship when we pray and **meditate.** We worship when we read and study the Bible. We worship when we sing hymns. We worship when we go to church. We worship when we give our money, time, and talents. We worship when we take Communion.

We can worship God when we are alone. Christians should take time to worship alone each day. We can also worship God with a group of people. Christians should worship **regularly** in a group. The Bible says, "Let us not **give up** meeting together . . ." (Hebrews 10:25) We grow and become strong Christians as we worship together.

Most Christians worship God on Sunday. This is a good day to worship God with other people. We go to church. We sing and pray. We hear our pastor preach from the Bible. We remember that Sunday is a special, holy day.

We eat food to have strong, healthy bodies. Food helps us grow. Christians worship to have strong, spiritual lives. Worship helps us grow as Christians. We know more about God when we worship Him. We should worship God each day.

QUESTIONS: *Fill In the blanks.*

1. Christians _____ the one true God.
2. We worship when we give _____ to God.
3. Christians should worship _____ alone each day.
4. Christians worship to have _____, _____ lives.
5. We should _____ God each day.

Give the answers.

6. What are two types of worship that are not right?

    (1) _____

    (2) _____

7. What are three ways we can worship God?

    (1) _____

    (2) _____

    (3) _____

8. Why should we worship together? Because we _____ and become _____ _____.

9. On what day of the week do many Christians worship together?

    _____

WORD LIST

1. **reverence** *(noun):* great love for God; obeying God; knowing that God is holy; thinking very much of God
2. **worthy** *(adjective):* most important; best of all
3. **meditate** *(verb):* think about
4. **regularly** *(adverb):* doing over and over again at set times
5. **give up** *(verb phrase):* stop

16 CHRISTIANS SHOULD JOIN A CHURCH

Scripture: Matthew 18:20

The church is a fellowship of Christian believers. The church is important to Christians. It is also a place for worship, fellowship, and serving God. It helps us grow in the family of God.

The church is where many people are saved. We go to church to learn about God. We learn about His plan of salvation. We accept His Son, Jesus Christ, as our Savior. We learn to live as Christians.

Christians should become church members. They should join a church. They should join a fellowship where the Bible is preached.

Here are some ways the church fellowship helps us:

1. The church helps us worship God. It has worship services for us to attend. We worship with other people. And Jesus Christ promises to be with us. He said, "For where two or three come together in My name, there am I with them." (Matthew 18:20)
2. The church helps us become friends with other Christians. These friends **encourage** us. And we encourage them. The Bible says, ". . . encourage one another and **build each other up** . . ." (1 Thessalonians 5:11) This is Christian fellowship.
3. The church helps us serve God. We give our tithes and offerings to God in church. We give Him our time and talents. We serve both God and people in church. The Bible says, ". . . serve the Lord with all your heart." (1 Samuel 12:20) ". . . serve one another in love." (Galatians 5:13)
4. The church helps us learn about the Christian life. We can attend Sunday school classes to study the Bible. Sometimes there are other Bible studies or meetings. We grow as we study and learn with other people. This helps us become stronger Christians.
5. The church helps us be true to God. The church has rules to guide us as Christians. The rules help us not to get hurt. They also help us not to hurt other people. The rules are for our good. They help us not to sin.

Are you a church member? Did you answer "no"? Then you should talk with your pastor. You need to join a church fellowship.

Did you answer "yes"? Good! You should attend church regularly and grow in the Lord.

QUESTIONS: *Fill In the blanks.*

1. The church is a _____ of Christian believers.
2. The church is where many people are _____.
3. Christians should become _____ _____.
4. The church helps us _____ God.
5. The church helps us become _____ with other Christians. We _____ each other.
6. The church helps us _____ God. We also serve _____.
7. The church helps us learn about the _____ _____.
8. The church helps us be _____ to God.
9. The _____ of the church are for our good.
10. We should _____ church regularly and _____ in the Lord.

WORD LIST

1. **encourage** *(verb):* give hope to; give help to
2. **build each other up** *(verb phrase):* encourage people; help people grow as Christians

17 CHRISTIANS GROW IN THE FAMILY OF GOD

Scripture: 1 John 3:2

Christians are children of God. The Bible says, ". . . we are children of God . . ." (1 John 3:2) God has made us a part of His family. This happens when we are **born again.** Jesus said, ". . . You must be born again." (John 3:7)

A baby starts to grow when he or she is born. But the baby needs good food. He or she needs care and love. The baby will not grow if he or she is **neglected.**

Christians need to grow after they are born again. God, our Father, wants His children to grow. He loves us very much. He cares for us. So He helps us in many ways. He does not neglect His children.

We have learned in this book about growing as a Christian. We have learned many ways God helps us. Now, let us **review** what these ways are.

The most important way is giving our will to God. We choose to do the will of God. His will becomes more important than our will. The Holy Spirit **cleanses** us from sin. And He fills our lives with His presence.

The Holy Spirit is a gift of God to us. The Holy Spirit is our Helper. He helps us grow.

We grow as Christians when we do these things:
1. We are baptized by our pastor.
2. We read and study the Bible.
3. We pray every day.
4. We give our tithes and offerings to God.
5. We give our time and talents to God.
6. We serve God by serving other people.
7. We tell other people what God has done for us.
8. We obey God and do what He tells us.
9. We avoid the things that do not honor God.
10. We take Communion when we can.
11. We worship God with other Christians and alone.
12. We join a church and share in its fellowship.

The Christian life is the best life. We have the love of God, our Father. We have the gift of eternal life through Jesus Christ. And, we have the help of the Holy Spirit every day.

We also have the love of other Christians. They give us their **support.** They are our brothers and sisters in Christ. We are all a part of the family of God.

Will you pray this prayer of **thanksgiving** and **commitment?**

Dear God, I thank You that I am Your child. I am so glad I belong to You. I am glad I have been born again. Thank You for showing me Your will for my life. Thank You for **cleansing** me from all sin. And thank You that the Holy Spirit is my Helper.

I also thank You for my church family. I am glad I have many brothers and sisters in You. Help us to encourage one another. Thank You for my pastor. Help him [her] as he [she] preaches each week. Give him [her] Your **wisdom** as he [she] helps Your children.

I am Yours, God. Please use me. Help me to keep growing. Help me to grow and become a strong Christian. Help me remember all the things I should do. And help me avoid the things I should not do. Help me live for You all my life.

I love You, Father. I pray this in Jesus' Name. Amen.

WORD LIST

1. **born again** *(verb phrase):* saved from sin; become a Christian or believer
2. **neglected** *(verb):* not cared for
3. **review** *(verb):* study again; remember again
4. **cleanses** *(verb):* makes clean; purifies
5. **support** *(noun):* care and love; all the ways Christians help each other
6. **thanksgiving** *(noun):* thanking someone; giving thanks to God
7. **commitment** *(noun):* giving yourself to God
8. **cleansing** *(verb):* making clean; purifying
9. **wisdom** *(noun):* what a person knows; using what you know in the best way

TEACHING RESOURCES

The lessons in this book, *How Christians Grow—In Beginning English,* and in its companion volume, *What Christians Believe—In Beginning English,* have been developed for adults who are limited in their English proficiency: refugees, new immigrants, bilingual speakers, and ESL (English as a second language) learners. Such people, who are just beginning to learn and study English and who are attending Christian churches, need materials in English with controlled vocabulary and sentence structure in order to help them understand the major doctrines of the Christian faith.

The lessons have been written with careful consideration to the vocabulary and sentence structure. A list of 1,000 words, based upon research from the fields of education and religion, served as the basis for the vocabulary control. Guidelines for language composition, based upon current educational and linguistic principles, served as the basis for the sentence structure control.

A few vocabulary items, words not in the 1,000-word list, have been introduced in each lesson. The new vocabulary, however, has been limited, averaging seven per lesson in this book.

In applying the necessary linguistic controls, the language has been greatly simplified. The writers have purposely sacrificed style for simplicity in order to obtain English at a level which is more easily read and understood by the intended audience.

The Christian truths introduced in this volume have been arranged in the order the writers felt were needed by the target audience. Other biblical truths were dealt with in the preceding volume, *What Christians Believe—In Beginning English.*

We believe this book meets a vital need that exists today in evangelical Christianity. We pray that God will honor His Word as it becomes a part of the learners' minds—and hearts—through the medium of beginning English.

ESL Advisory Committee for
Publications International

J. Wesley Eby, Chairperson
Nancy Clark
Nancy Zumwalt

APPENDIX A
WORD LIST: NEW VOCABULARY

Below is an alphabetical list of all the words and phrases in the Word Lists in this book. The numbers following each entry indicate the lessons where the words were introduced.

avoid *(verb)*: keep away from; not do at all (8)

backslide *(verb)*: to neglect doing the will of God; to choose to disobey God; to turn from following Jesus Christ (11)

backsliding *(noun)*: neglecting to do the will of God; choosing our will, not the will of God; choosing not to follow Jesus Christ (11)

Bible study *(noun phrase)*: learning what is in the Bible; learning what the Bible says to us (3)

bless *(verb)*: make happy; give joy to (5)

born again *(verb phrase)*: saved from sin; become a Christian or believer (17)

broken *(verb)*: hurt; death (12)

build each other up *(verb phrase)*: encourage people; help people grow as Christians (16)

cheerful *(adjective)*: happy; glad (5)

choices *(noun)*: acts of choosing or deciding something; when we decide between two or more things (3)

cleanses *(verb)*: makes clean; purifies (17)

cleansing *(verb)*: making clean; purifying (17)

commitment *(noun)*: giving yourself to God (17)

completely *(adverb)*: all; in whole; with everything (10)

consecrated *(adjective)*: given to God (10)

consecrates *(verb)*: gives something to God to be used only by God (10)

consecration *(noun)*: the act of giving something to God (10)

continually *(adverb)*: all the time; never stops (14)

convict *(verb)*: make known; help people to know about (9)

counselor *(noun)*: a person who listens to our problems; a person who helps us with our problems (9)

decision *(noun)*: what you decide to do; what you choose to do (1)

devotions *(noun)*: a time of prayer, Bible study, and thinking about God (14)

difficult world *(noun phrase)*: not easy to live in; hard to live in; a world full of sin and wrong (1)

disciples *(noun)*: believers; people who follow Jesus Christ (2)

elders *(noun)*: important leaders in a church (13)

emotions *(noun)*: our feelings, such as love, hate, fear, joy, etc. (13)

enemies *(noun)*: people who are not friends; people who hate and hurt other people (6)

encourage *(verb)*: give hope to; give help to (16)

entire sanctification *(noun phrase)*: the special act of God that makes Christians pure and holy; this happens after people are saved (10)

eternal life *(noun phrase)*: the life God gives; the good life with God now and life with God forever (3)

example *(noun)*: shows one of a kind of something; an example helps us to know better what something means or is (5)

faithful *(adjective):* always doing what you should be doing; full of faith (4)
feel His presence *(verb phrase):* know God is present; know God is near (14)
fellowship *(noun):* being friends; loving and caring for each other (11)
forgiveness *(noun):* God choosing to forgive our sins (4)

gave thanks *(verb phrase):* prayed; thanked God for; prayed before eating a meal (12)
givers *(noun):* people who give something; people who give money to God (5)
give up *(verb phrase):* stop
gospel *(noun):* the story of salvation from sin through Jesus Christ; this story is told in
    Matthew, Mark, Luke, and John; these four books are called the Gospels (7)
gradually *(adverb):* slow change; not fast; not happening all at one time (13)
grow as a Christian *(verb phrase):* to learn more about the Christian life; to be more like
    Jesus Christ (1)

happiness *(noun):* being happy and glad; full of joy (7)
harmful *(adjective):* full of harm; that which hurts us; that which makes us sin (8)
healthy *(adjective):* not sick; being well in the body (3)
honest *(adjective):* true; right (4)
honor *(verb):* worship; obey; give a high place to (8)
hymns *(noun):* songs which praise and worship God (4)

immediately *(adverb):* right away; done at once; happens with no waiting (13)
in remembrance of *(prepositional phrase):* to remember; to think of again (12)

janitors *(noun):* people who clean and take care of buildings (8)

knowledge *(noun):* what a person knows; what a person has learned (1)

lonely *(adjective):* feeling all alone; feeling no one cares about you (6)
Lord's Day *(proper noun phrase):* Sunday; the day most Christians worship God (8)

medicine *(noun):* what doctors give to help make people well (13)
meditate *(verb):* think about (15)
memorize *(verb):* learn something so you can remember it (4)
minister *(noun):* a preacher who serves God and people in the church (2)
myself *(pronoun):* I; me (10)

neglect *(verb):* to not do; to not care for (11)
neglected *(verb):* not cared for (17)
non-Christians *(noun):* people who are not Christians; people who do not believe in Jesus
    Christ (6)

offerings *(noun):* gifts given to God, usually money (5)

pastor *(noun):* the minister or preacher in a church (13)
please *(verb):* to make someone happy; to make God happy (8)
poured out *(verb phrase):* given; spilled; shed (12)
provide a way out *(verb phrase):* make us strong; help us not to yield; help us not to sin (11)
purifies *(verb):* makes pure and clean; makes holy (10)

regularly *(adverb):* doing over and over again at set times (15)
represent *(verb):* to mean; to show (12)
reverence *(noun):* great love for God; obeying God; knowing that God is holy; thinking
    very much of God (15)
review *(verb):* study again; remember again (17)

sacred *(adjective):* belongs to God; holy (8)

sanctifies *(verb):* makes pure and holy; sets apart for a holy reason (10)

saved *(verb):* made free or safe from sin; freed from the power of sin in our lives (2)

separation *(noun):* not together; apart (2)

servants *(noun):* people who serve God and other people; people who work for God (6)

service *(noun):* a time when Christians meet together to worship God (12)

sex sins *(noun phrase):* wrong sex; all sex that is not between a man and his wife (8)

sharing and caring *(noun phrase):* helping people; letting people know you want to help them in any way you can; giving to other people a part of what you have; being friends with people (14)

shed *(verb):* given; spilled; poured out (12)

sickness *(noun):* being sick; not well (13)

slaves to sin *(noun phrase):* people who are sinners; people who are controlled by sin (2)

Son of Man *(proper noun phrase):* Jesus Christ (6)

spirit *(noun):* the real self; what a person is inside his being (9)

Spirit *(proper noun):* the Holy Spirit; the Spirit of God (9)

spiritual *(adjective):* things of God; things of the Holy Spirit (3)

sprinkled *(verb):* shake small drops of water on (2)

storehouse *(noun):* the church or place where you worship God (5)

strength *(noun):* power; help (13)

supply *(verb):* give what is needed (4)

support *(noun):* care and love; all the ways Christians help each other (17)

talents *(noun):* the things people do very well; what people are able to do very well (5)

telephone *(noun):* a tool we use to talk with people away from us; we can hear them but cannot see them (14)

temples *(noun):* places of worship; places where the Spirit of God lives (8)

temptation *(noun):* the act of being tempted by Satan; Satan trying to get a person to do wrong and disobey God (11)

Ten Commandments *(proper noun phrase):* ten important laws or rules that God gave to His people (See Exodus 20:2-17) (8)

testifies *(verb):* makes us know; agrees with (9)

testify *(verb):* tell other people what God has done for you (14)

thanksgiving *(noun):* thanking someone; giving thanks to God (17)

through and through *(adverb phrase):* in whole; completely; from top to bottom; from one side to the other side (10)

tithe *(noun):* one part of ten; money given to God through the church (5)

triune *(adjective):* God is God in three persons: God the Father, God the Son, and God the Holy Spirit (1)

true *(adjective):* faithful; always doing what you should be doing; always obeying God (11)

victory over sin *(noun phrase):* have no sin; obey God in all things (9)

will *(noun):* the power to choose; to decide between two or more things (10)

will of God *(noun phrase):* what God wants for people (10)

wisdom *(noun):* what a person knows; using what you know in the best way (17)

witness *(verb):* tell people about Jesus Christ; tell what Jesus Christ has done for you (5)

witnessing *(noun):* sharing or telling other people about something good; telling other people about God and His Son, Jesus Christ (7)

wonderful *(adjective):* great; very, very good (1)

worthy *(adjective):* most important; best of all (15)

yield *(verb):* to do the thing we should not do; to say "yes" to sin (11)

APPENDIX B

Answers to Questions and Additional Scripture References

The information in this appendix is provided to help the teacher in teaching the 17 lessons in this book.

For each lesson, there is a set of suggested answers for the study questions. You will find the intended answers, along with some possible alternatives (in parentheses), which are all correct in the context of the lessons. Teachers should be willing to accept any answer that can be justified.

There is also a list of additional Scripture references for each lesson. These will provide biblical support for the Christian beliefs and practices that are presented. Teachers may use these for background reading as well as in the teaching of the lessons. A student who is literate in a language other than English will benefit from reading these Scripture verses in his or her own Bible.

LESSON 1

Answers to Questions:

1. learn
2. true (triune)
3. answers
4. Bible
5. sinners
6. heaven
7. God
8. Believers (Christians)
9. (personal response)
10. (personal response)
11. (personal response)
12. (personal response)

Additional Scripture References:

Matthew 5:1 - 7:29
   (Sermon on the Mount)
John 15:1-8
Romans 12:1-21
1 Corinthians 13:47
Philippians 1:9-11
Philippians 3:12-16
Colossians 1:10
Colossians 3:17
1 Thessalonians 4:7-8
2 Thessalonians 1:3
2 Timothy 2:22
Hebrews 12:14
1 Peter 1:15-16
2 Peter 1:5-9

LESSON 2

Answers to Questions:

1. repent
2. sin
3. saved
4. believe; Jesus Christ
5. baptized
6. Jesus Christ
7. all Christians
8. a minister
9. can watch

Additional Scripture References:

Matthew 3:1-6; 11
Matthew 28:19-20
Acts 2:38, 41
Acts 8:12
Acts 8:38
Acts 10:47-48
Acts 19:4-5
Acts 22:16
Romans 6:3-4
Galatians 3:26-27
1 Peter 3:21

LESSON 3

Answers to Questions:

1. (Holy) Bible
2. God better
3. read; study
4. truth
5. live
6. better Christians
7. Jesus Christ
8. sin; wrong
9. God (Jesus Christ; Holy spirit)
10. (the Holy) Bible

Additional Scripture References:

Deuteronomy 6:6
Joshua 1:8
Psalm 1:2
Psalm 19:7-11
Psalm 33:4
Psalm 119:9-11
Psalm 119:105-106
Psalm 119:129-130
Isaiah 40:8
Mark 13:31
Luke 11:28
John 8:32
John 17:17
Ephesians 6:13-17
2 Timothy 2:15
2 Timothy 3:15-17
Hebrews 4:12
2 Peter 1:20-21

LESSON 4

Answers to Questions:

1. Prayer
2. words; thoughts
3. God
4. given to you
5. forgiveness
6. prayers; right
7. at any time
8. our needs
9. God
10. the Lord's Prayer

Additional Scripture References:

Deuteronomy 4:7
2 Chronicles 7:14
Psalm 4:1
Psalm 66:20
Proverbs 15:8
Jeremiah 29:12-13
Matthew 6:5-8
Matthew 21:22
Mark 11:24-25
Romans 8:26-27
Ephesians 1:17-18
Ephesians 6:18-20
Philippians 4:6
Colossians 4:2
1 Thessalonians 5:17
James 5:16
1 Peter 3:12

LESSON 5

Answers to Questions:

1. serving
2. tithe
3. love God
4. give
5. tithe; offerings; time; talents
6. the church (the place where you worship God)
7. God (the Lord)
8. cheerful (happy)
9. talents
10. Any three of the following are acceptable:
    (1) pray (every day)
    (2) study the Bible (every day)
    (3) go to church
    (4) witness to other people
    (5) help other people (help them)

Additional Scripture References:

Genesis 28:22
Numbers 18:21
Deuteronomy 12:17
Deuteronomy 15:10-11
2 Chronicles 31:5
Nehemiah 10:37
Proverbs 21:26
Malachi 3:8-10
Matthew 10:8
Matthew 22:21
Luke 6:38
Acts 20:35
Romans 12:8
1 Corinthians 16:2
2 Corinthians 9:6-8
Philippians 4:15-19

LESSON 6

Answers to Questions:

1. servants
2. serve
3. many ways (many places)
4. church; away
5. they love God
6. Jesus Christ
7. (Any of the following answers are correct.) have Bible studies; cook meals for other people; care for sick people; visit non-Christians and witness to them; help poor or lonely people; be kind to enemies
8. God

Additional Scripture References:

Deuteronomy 10:12-13
Joshua 22:5
Joshua 24:14-15
1 Samuel 12:24
Matthew 6:24
Matthew 20:26-28
Matthew 25:21
Mark 10:43-45
John 12:26
Romans 12:6-8
1 Corinthians 12:4-11
1 Corinthians 14:12
Galatians 5:13-14
Ephesians 6:7-8
Philippians 2:5-8
1 Peter 4:10-11

LESSON 7

Answers to Questions:

1. Jesus Christ
2. forgiveness
3. disciples; love
4. witnesses
5. afraid
6. done for them
7. acts; words
8. Jesus Christ (God)
9. good

Additional Scripture References:

Psalm 107:2
Proverbs 12:17
Matthew 5:14-16
Matthew 28:16-20
Mark 8:38
John 15:26-27
Romans 1:16
Romans 12:9-21
Romans 13:8-10
1 Corinthians 13:4
Galatians 5:22-26
Ephesians 4:32
Colossians 3:13
1 Thessalonians 5:15
2 Timothy 1:8
2 Timothy 2:24
1 John 5:9-12
Revelation 12:11

LESSON 8

Answers to Questions:

1. please God
2. name of God
3. hurt (harm)
4. everything
5. holy, pure

6. do not please God
7. (the Holy) Bible
8. the Lord's Day (Sunday)
9. Jesus Christ (God)
10. bodies; minds; words; deeds

Additional Scripture References:

Leviticus 19:12
Proverbs 20:1
Isaiah 28:1, 7-8
Isaiah 58:13-14
Matthew 5:27-28
Matthew 5:34-37
Acts 20:7
Romans 12:17-18
1 Corinthians 6:9
1 Corinthians 6:18-20

2 Corinthians 7:1
Galatians 5:13-15
Ephesians 4:32
Ephesians 5:18
1 Thessalonians 4:3-7
2 Timothy 2:23-24
James 3:5-6
James 4:4
1 Peter 3:8-11

LESSON 9

Answers to Questions:

1. God
2. Jesus Christ
3. lives
4. Counselor
5. problems

6. (the) Holy Spirit
7. convict; sin
8. Christians
9. (the) Holy Spirit
10. sin

Additional Scripture References:

Matthew 3:16-17
John 7:39
John 14:15-18
John 16:7-15
Acts 1:4-5, 8
Acts 2:4
Acts 2:33
Acts 15:8

Romans 8:1-27
Galatians 4:6
Ephesians 3:16-17
1 Thessalonians 4:7-8
2 Thessalonians 2:13
1 John 3:24
1 John 4:13

LESSON 10

Answers to Questions:

1. best (will)
2. way (will)
3. choose
4. will
5. Holy Spirit
6. love God (obey God)
7. consecrated
8. sanctify
9. filled
10. do

Additional Scripture References:

Ezekiel 36:25-27
Matthew 3:11
Matthew 5:8
Matthew 5:48
John 17:16-19
Acts 1:5
Acts 2:1-4
Acts 15:8-9
Romans 6:11-14
Romans 8:8-11
Romans 12:1-2

2 Corinthians 7:1
Galatians 2:20
Galatians 5:16-25
Ephesians 5:17-18
1 Thessalonians 4:7
2 Thessalonians 2:13
Hebrews 12:14
Hebrews 13:12
1 Peter 1:15-16
1 John 1:9

LESSON 11

Answers to Questions:

1. child of God
2. neglect
3. separate; fellowship
4. Temptation
5. yield
6. sin
7. forgive
8. backslide
9. Holy Spirit

Additional Scripture References:

2 Chronicles 7:14
Psalm 51:1-12
Jeremiah 2:19
Jeremiah 3:22
Jeremiah 14:7
Ezekiel 37:23
Hosea 14:4
Matthew 4:1-11
Matthew 6:13

Matthew 26:41
Luke 22:40
Acts 13:38-39
Romans 7:21-26
Galatians 6:1
Ephesians 1:7
Hebrews 2:18
Hebrews 4:14-16
James 1:13-15

LESSON 12

Answers to Questions:

1. Lord's Supper
2. believers (Christians)
3. gave thanks
4. bread
5. juice (made from grapes)
6. (His) blood
7. death; Jesus
8. comes again

Additional Scripture References:

Exodus 12:1-14
Matthew 26:17-29
Mark 14:12-25
Luke 22:7-20

John 6:53-58
1 Corinthians 10:14-21
1 Corinthians 11:23-29

LESSON 13

Answers to Questions:

1. bodies; minds; emotions
2. sick people
3. great power
4. heal
5. doctors; medicine
6. choose
7. Sickness
8. God (Jesus Christ)
9. pastor; elders
10. everything

Additional Scripture References:

2 Kings 5:1-15
Psalm 103:2-3
Isaiah 53:4-5
Matthew 4:23-24
Matthew 9:18-35
Matthew 10:1,8

John 4:46-54
Acts 5:12-16
Romans 8:28
1 Corinthians 12:4-11
2 Corinthians 12:7-10
James 5:13-16

LESSON 14

Answers to Questions:

1. fellowship; worship
2. testify
3. sharing; caring
4. love; caring
5. God
6. devotions
7. presence
8. (Any answers from numbers 1-6 in the lesson are correct. Other answers may also be correct.)
9. Father; Jesus Christ
10. (Christian) fellowship

Additional Scripture References:

Proverbs 14:21,31
Matthew 22:37-39
Matthew 25:34-40
Acts 9:36
Acts 20:35
Romans 12:6-8,10,13
1 Corinthians 1:9
1 Corinthians 12:28
2 Corinthians 13:14
Galatians 2:9-10
Philippians 2:1-4
Philippians 3:10
1 Thessalonians 5:11
Hebrews 3:13
Hebrews 10:24-25
James 4:8
1 John 1:3-7

LESSON 15

Answers to Questions:

1. worship
2. praise (money; time; talents; etc.)
3. God
4. strong; spiritual
5. worship
6. false gods; other people; money; jobs; things we own; etc.
7. (There are many possible answers. Accept all that fit the context of the lesson.)
8. grow; strong Christians
9. Sunday

Additional Scripture References:

1 Chronicles 16:29
2 Chronicles 7:3
Psalm 19:14
Psalm 29:2
Psalm 95:6-7
Psalm 100:2
Psalm 119:97
Matthew 6:6
John 4:24
Romans 12:1
Ephesians 5:19-20
Philippians 3:3
Colossians 3:16
Hebrews 3:1
Revelation 14:7

LESSON 16

Answers to Questions:

1. fellowship
2. saved
3. church members
4. worship
5. friends; encourage (build up)
6. serve; people (one another)
7. Christian life
8. true
9. rules
10. attend; grow

Additional Scripture References:

Psalm 122:1
Acts 2:41-42; 46-47
Romans 12:4-8
1 Corinthians 12:12-31
1 Corinthians 14:12
1 Corinthians 14:26

Ephesians 4:11-13
Ephesians 4:25
Ephesians 5:22-30
Colossians 1:18
Hebrews 10:25

LESSON 17

Answers to Questions: (none)

Additional Scripture References:

John 1:12-13
John 3:3-8
Romans 8:16
Colossians 1:10
2 Thessalonians 1:3
Hebrews 5:11-14
1 Peter 1:23

1 Peter 2:2
2 Peter 3:18
1 John 3:1
1 John 3:9
1 John 4:7
1 John 5:1-5
1 John 5:18-19

APPENDIX C
TIPS FOR TEACHING ESL

A. **Plan carefully and prayerfully.** Anything important enough to do is important enough to *plan* to do. Unplanned teaching usually means disconnected, haphazard instruction, resulting in limited, minimal learning. *Remember:* "if we fail to plan, we plan to fail."

Your students are worthy of your careful planning and *sincere prayers.* Commit your "situation"—the learners, the lessons, the results—to Him. God will be faithful to help you as you do your best.

B. **Be sensitive to the learners' needs.** Your students will probably be at different levels, both in their language learning and in their knowledge of the Bible. Your task—a difficult one, for sure—is to discover "where" the learners are in their English levels and their understanding of the Christian faith.

Be aware, also, that the learners' *felt needs* may be different from their *real needs;* but their *felt needs* usually must be met first before you are able to help them with their *real needs.* For example, a person's medical concerns may need attention before he/she is ready to hear about God or learn the English language. In your class, you may find that the *felt need* is to learn English while the *real need* is to learn about God.

There is no magic formula to help you in making this discovery. However, you need to become a "people-watcher" and look for any cues the students may give in their body language and facial expressions as well as in what they say. Also, your involvement in the learners' lives, both in and out of class, will certainly help you to be much more aware of their backgrounds, their culture, their experiences, and, thus, their needs—*felt* and *real.* Again, God will be faithful as you commit this "discovery process" to Him.

C. **Determine your objective.** An objective is the purpose for teaching. Your objective, as a Christian ESL teacher, is actually twofold: the Christian faith and the English language. Knowing *what* you are teaching, and *why,* will undoubtedly help you to be more confident, and your instruction will certainly be more effective. It is important, therefore, that you become familiar with two things: first, the lesson content, and second, if possible, the vocabulary and sentence structure being taught.

D. **Focus on comprehension.** This is essential! If the learners do not understand, your instruction will be fruitless. Naturally, every student will not fully understand everything you teach. Yet, as a teacher, you should endeavor to have each student "take away" some learning from each session. How much is understood and learned will vary, of course, from student to student. But, as you faithfully plant the seeds of God's Word, the Holy Spirit will help those seeds to grow and bear fruit in the minds and hearts of the learners.

Some strategies for aiding comprehension are:

1. If you speak the students' language or if an interpreter is available, teach the lessons bilingually. This is ideal and will result in the greatest amount of learning.

2. Have the students read the Scripture in their own language, if possible. This will certainly aid their understanding. God says, ". . . My Word . . . will not return to Me empty, but will accomplish what I desire and achieve the purpose for which I sent it" (Isaiah 55:11, NIV).

   Two excellent sources of Bibles in various languages are:
   - The American Bible Society, 1865 Broadway, New York, NY 10023
   - Gideons International (Contact a local Gideons organization in your area.)

3. Take additional time to teach a lesson, as needed. You can divide a lesson into two or more parts, according to the needs of the learners. However, it is not recommended that the lessons be taught in more than three or four sessions, especially if the class sessions are only once a week.

4. The questions are an important part of each lesson. If time permits, you should use the questions as an integral part of your teaching. Or, if time is limited, the questions can be assigned for home study and discussed during the next class session as review and reinforcement. *Note:* It is recommended that you avoid "grading" the students' answers in such a way that the students have a sense of failure. (See Section E.)

5. Do not assume that the learners can read at a second grade reading level (the level at which these lessons have been written according to the Fry readability scale). If the learners cannot read English, the lessons can be taught orally. The amount of *reading* that you teach, of course, will be determined by your skills in the teaching of reading. Yet, whatever your skill level, do not be afraid to try.

   Once your students are apparently reading the lessons on their own, do not automatically assume they understand what they are reading just because they can pronounce the words. Use questions and discussion to help you determine their degree of comprehension.

6. Do not assume that the learners know all the words in the 1,000-word vocabulary list used in writing these lessons. You may need to work with the "unknown" words both before and during the teaching of the lessons.

7. Develop vocabulary in meaningful situations. Never use isolated word lists. Many of the high frequency words of English, such as articles, auxiliaries, prepositions, and conjunctions, have limited or no meaning in and by themselves. In addition, many of the content words, such as nouns, verbs, adjectives, and adverbs, have multiple meanings. Therefore, vocabulary instruction has little value if there is no useful meaning attached to the words for the learners involved. Always work with unknown words in phrases or sentences that have meaning for your particular students. Also, be very careful in the use of idioms, figures of speech, and slang expressions as they are difficult for ESL learners to comprehend.

8. Add your own examples and illustrations appropriate for the lessons. Examples and illustrations have not been included since they are culture-specific and the lessons are designed to be used in all cultures. Yet, the writers recognize that appropriate stories or examples are very effective and essential in the learning process. *Caution:* Make certain the stories, examples, or illustrations are appropriate and meaningful for the learners you are teaching.

9. As much as possible, make extensive use of real objects, pictures, and other audiovisual aids. Bulletin boards, charts, flash cards, cassette tapes, etc. can help you to teach the lessons more effectively.

E. **Teach for success.** This begins, of course, with focusing on comprehension. If the learners understand, then success is a natural by-product.

The following should be observed in teaching for success:

1. Give frequent, *sincere* praise. An absolute must!

2. Capitalize on the learners' strengths and their correct responses, while minimizing their weaknesses and mistakes.

3. Assume every student *wants* to learn, *can* learn, and *will* learn. Then, teach accordingly. *Remember:* negative attitudes are always "caught."

F. **Be a "good" language model.** This is critical since language is introduced through the ear. Being a language model, however, does not mean you have to be perfect; therefore, you can discard your apprehensions.

Here are some tips that will help you:

1. *Be natural.* Use spoken English as it is naturally used by native English speakers. Be extremely careful not to "talk down" to the learners by using "baby talk" or "Tarzan-type" language (e.g., "Me Tarzan. You Jane.").

2. *Talk slowly.* Second language learners find English easier to understand if it is spoken somewhat slower than the normal speech of native speakers. Yet, the speaker must maintain appropriate volume, rhythm,

stress, and phrasing. *Caution:* Do not slow down to the point of producing distorted or unnatural language.

A common mistake made by many novice ESL teachers is to increase their volume as they slow down their speech. ESL learners are not hard-of-hearing; thus, when English speakers increase their volume, it is often viewed by others as "talking down" to them. *Caution:* Be aware of your volume level as you teach your students.

3. *Enunciate clearly.* Be distinct in pronouncing your words, making certain that final consonant sounds are not omitted or slurred. Try to be clear and precise in your pronunciation while retaining naturalness.

Do not expect adults or older youth who are learning English as a second language to speak it as native speakers. Research indicates that they will always, in all likelihood, speak it with an accent.

4. *Model correct language.* This is an important technique for all teaching, and especially for correcting mistakes. You can demonstrate the correct response, appropriate language usage, or pronunciation simply by "doing it" yourself.

Do not require the students to correct all their mistakes. For each lesson, focus on only one or two mistakes you would like them to correct and master. Focusing on too many errors at once can be discouraging and embarrassing for any learner.

5. *Read aloud often.* You, as the teacher, can model good reading and oral language as you read aloud to the students. Current research indicates that this is an important technique to be used with any learner of any age. And as you read, be expressive and enthusiastic.

ESL students need to hear you frequently read the Bible as well as the entire lesson. In fact, it is recommended that you read each lesson to the students first before they ever see it. Then, read it a second time while they follow along with their eyes. This provides them with the needed auditory (ear) and visual (eye) introduction to the lesson before they read it on their own.

EDITOR'S NOTE:

The information provided in this appendix on teaching English as a second language (ESL) is extremely limited. Entire textbooks have been written and devoted to this subject. However, space requirements in this book necessitate that this supplementary material be concise and limited. I pray, though, that what you have read in this brief treatment on teaching ESL will be of assistance to you as you minister to people with limited English proficiency.

J. Wesley Eby